The Smell of Summer

A SMELLS OF THE SEASONS BOOK
A blind girl experiences the season through her nose.

by Mary Ann Hake

Illustrated by Marina at GetYourBookIllustrations

To my dear mother, Isabelle Schmidt Ostermann, who always encouraged my writing.

— M.A.H. (her only summer child)

Copyright © 2023 Mary Ann Hake

Loving Hope Publishing

All rights reserved. This book or any portion thereafter may not be reproduced or used in any manner whatsoever without the express written permission of the publishers except for the use of brief quotations in a book review.

ISBN: 979-8-9880428-0-8   (Ebook)
ISBN: 979-8-9880428-2-2   (Hardback)
ISBN: 979-8-9880428-1-5   (Paperback)

Illustrated by Marina at GetYourBookIllustrations
Cover and Book Design by Kezia at GetYourBookIllustrations
www.getyourbookillustrations.com

First Print 2023

As summer thoughts stir in my mind,
I wonder what new smells I'll find.
Since noses surely help us see,
What special scents will call to me?

Warm summer sun awakes fresh scents.
The flowers wave along the fence
As blossoms burst with rich perfume—
A different fragrance gifts each bloom.

The buzzing bees sip nectar sweet
And make their honey for a treat.
A bee man has a fragrant task.
Can he smell honey through his mask?

Then Muffy reeks damp doggy wet
As drops now splatter from my pet.

The heat sure makes me stink with sweat,
So I will find a different wet.
It's time to jump in some place cool—
The strong aroma of my pool.

I swim, and Dad comes out to grill.
Soon yummy smells the air will fill—
Fresh burgers and corn on the cob
Delighting noses with his job.

Our garden's bounty we will share,
And enter veggies at the fair.
Tomatoes, carrots, beans, and beets—
Their scents sure draw me to these treats.

Along the woodchip-covered trail,
Whiffs guide my nose to food for sale:
Fried treats, popcorn, cotton candy.
Noses sure do come in handy.

A zoo holds some exotic smells.
The musk ox odor always tells.
An elephant's long trunk can snuff,
But my small nose is quite enough.

I like to go play at the beach
And walk above the sea spray's reach.
Wet sand sends up a salty scent
When waves are splashing or all spent.

I smell the seaweed on the shore,
A fishy odor near the store,
The stinky seals on wooden docks,
And sea anemone on rocks.

While camping near a forest stream,
The scents of nature fill my dream
With fragrant woodsmoke from our fire
And all the s'mores that I desire.

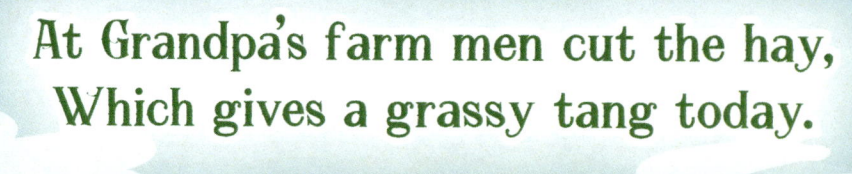

At Grandpa's farm men cut the hay,
Which gives a grassy tang today.

I sniff a pleasant fruit surprise.
My grandma's baking berry pies.

A holiday picnic's food smells great.
Then fireworks blast to celebrate.
A burnt smell lingers in the air
Reminding us to take great care.

I love the many summer smells.
So many stories each one tells.
Smells in the air and on the ground—
These smells may be the best I've found.

Author Bio

Mary Ann Hake's first picture book, *The Smell of Spring*, received the prestigious Mom's Choice Award. She has always loved learning and has been scribbling stories and poems since she first learned to write. Hundreds of her stories, articles, poems, puzzles, devotions, curricula, and more (for both children and adults) can be found in periodicals and books plus hundreds of book reviews online. She previously worked in a bookstore and as a librarian and enjoyed reading to children at story times and conducting the summer reading program. She has also taught writing to children and at writers' conferences. In addition to reading and writing, she continues to work as a freelance editor. Visit her website at www.maryannhake.com and sign up for her monthly newsletter and get activities with the sense of smell. Find her on Facebook at Mary A. Hake author.

Further Activities Using the Sense of Smell

Here are some smelly games:

Take turns listing summer smells.

Try to name a smell for each letter of the alphabet.

Have one person hide "smells" in small bags or boxes. The others take turns sniffing and guessing what each smell without peeking inside. (You may use a blindfold.)
Ideas for scented objects to hide: a lemon or an orange, peppermint, chocolate, an onion or garlic, a rose, cinnamon, licorice, mustard, ketchup, hot sauce, pepper, dirt.
[Another way to play this game is to use cotton balls scented with essential oils or extracts. Place each in a small sealed container. Number each container, and list the smell of each cotton ball for an answer key.]

Made in the USA
Middletown, DE
13 April 2024